Wings of Soul

Wings of Soul

Releasing Your Spiritual Identity

The World and Wisdom of

Dadi Janki

Health Communications, Inc.
Deerfield Beach, Florida

www.hci-online.com

Library of Congress Cataloging-in-Publication Data

Janki, Dadi.

    Wings of soul : releasing your spiritual identity / Dadi Janki.

        p.   cm.

    Reprint. London, England : Brahma Kumaris Information Services, Global Co-operation House.

    ISBN 1-55874-672-2

    1. Spiritual life—Hinduism.   I. Title.

BL1237.32.J36   1999

294.5'44—dc21   99–10664

                                                           CIP

ISBN 1-55874-672-2

Originally published by Brahma Kumaris Information Services, Global Co-operation House, 65 Pound Lane, London NW10 2HH UK, in association with Brahma Kumaris World Spiritual University (UK) registered charity No. 269971. ISBN 1-886872-12-0 first published 1998.

Publisher: Health Communications, Inc.
              3201 S.W. 15th Street
              Deerfield Beach, FL 33442-8190

Artwork by Marie Binder

INTRODUCTION

Dadi Janki
Additional Administrative Head
Brahma Kumaris

Prajapita Brahma
Founder
Brahma Kumaris

Can words serve as wings? Great poetry uplifts the spirit; but this book aims to take the soul even higher, into a state of lasting happiness. The love and wisdom which shine through its pages are of divine origin, and it is the Divine alone that can teach us how to reach a place beyond sorrow.

Dadi Janki is a yogi—one who seeks union with God. Her life's work has been to build within herself the experience of the Divine, and to share that experience with the world. She is convinced that we do not need to suffer, and she has the courage to tell us so. With God's help, we can achieve such understanding of the self and others around us that burdens carried from the past can at last be put down, allowing our full potential to be restored.

Born in India in 1916 to a devout and philanthropic family,

Dadi Janki recalls childhood years filled with a longing to know and come close to God. In 1936, at the age of nineteen, she experienced this encounter directly. It happened through Prajapita Brahma, a former businessman who, following a series of extraordinary visions, had surrendered everything he had in order to found a new movement for world spiritual renewal.

Brahma Baba, as he affectionately became known, felt he had reached a low point in his own journey through time, but that the Supreme was now showing him how to uplift both himself and others. From the moment she met him, Dadi Janki knew she must follow the same Light, with the same dedication. Since then, hundreds of thousands of others, from a multitude of religious and social backgrounds, have set out on the same path, inspired by the example set by the founding members.

To keep heart and mind stable and still, and to be alert to the presence and guidance of the Divine, has been Dadi's top priority in life, and it is from this that so many practical achievements have sprung. Dadi has shown an unswerving concentration on the task of world change through self-change. She has acquired such pure motivation and positivity of character that in a world darkened by materialism, her thoughts and words sparkle like jewels.

This book is packed with a selection of those jewels—polished insights into the truth about the essentially spiritual nature of the self, and how that truth can be applied and sustained in everyday life. They are not to be marveled at from a distance, but used to decorate and transform our hearts and minds until, like Dadi Janki, we too can move through life as free angels, above yet not remote, detached yet loving, on wings of Soul.

THE BOOK

This book is a compilation of classes and public presentations given by Dadi Janki over a period of about ten years. These have been revised and edited with the aim of communicating the spirit, and not just the letter, of Dadi's words.

One of the first steps in creating this book has been to adapt Dadi's oral presentations to written text. The main challenge in this comes from the fact that Dadi hardly ever actually delivers a speech, or lectures as such—she never, for example, reads from any sort of prepared text. On the contrary, whether Dadi is addressing a room of nine or an auditorium of 900, her words flow with an ease that comes from the wisdom of her own personal experience. She speaks only from the heart. Nor does anyone attending any of her programs ever feel that they are hearing a lecture. They feel they are being mothered. Or that they are listening to a symphony. Or witnessing a dance—such is the fullness and beauty of what Dadi shares. How can that be recorded on paper?

It is for this reason that the book has made use of a half stanza, half poetry format. The idea is to create enough space around Dadi's words as to invite you, the reader, to go beyond her words into the vibration and intention that surround them.

It is the experience of everyone who knows her that when you allow yourself to do this while listening to Dadi, it is as if God Himself plucks just those chords in you that resonate with whatever she is relating. And you become more than just a listener. You become part of that symphony, that dance, yourself. My hope is that you will enjoy something of this feeling as you explore the pages of this book.

The beautiful paintings by French artist Marie Binder have been added with the same purpose in mind—to make accessible the full experience of Dadi's wisdom in a way that transcends a strictly left-brain approach. The subtleties in the drawings go a long way in inviting the right brain to participate in the process of understanding *through* the heart what Dadi is sharing *from* the heart.

As well as being a source of inspiration, Dadi is a master at removing mental and emotional obstacles to self-fulfillment. This book contains many of the tools needed to help with this process. I hope you will experiment with these tools and find them of as much practical value in your life as they have been in mine.

Additionally, Dadi's frequent use of the pronoun "He" in reference to God should not be misinterpreted as a gender-biased understanding of God. The teachings of Brahma Kumaris Raja Yoga are based on the experience of God as a non-physical Being, who is Supreme by virtue of His/Her perfect balance and degree of both masculine and feminine attributes. It is more for the sake of prose that the "He" pronoun has been used.

A lot of hands have gone into the making of this book. I would like to acknowledge the cooperation of all those who have contributed their time and ideas so generously.

Finally, I would like to express my gratitude, both to God and Dadi, for the wonderful opportunity of working on this book. It has been a joyful reinforcement of my ideals, serving to strengthen my own efforts towards world transformation via self-transformation.

The Editor

To God

Thank you for granting us
wings of soul and
inspiring our hearts to fly.

CONTENTS

2. God

3. The World

4. Meditation

5. The Art of Living

6. On Dadi's Personal Journey

Part C: Parting Vision

Part A

Prelude Vision

HUMILITY AND EMPOWERMENT

Part One

I The Power of Truth

The power of Truth is such that you need never be concerned about proving it.

Trying to prove Truth reveals only your own stubbornness.

You need only be concerned with being it and living it, your own self.

Truth is always revealed, at the right moment, at the right place.

It is for this reason that the simplest, most powerful expression of Truth is Humility.

II   Simplicity

Humility makes you simple and truthful.

The more humility you have, the greater will be your understanding of truth.

And vice versa.

III   Self-Respect

Self-respect is a state of inner dignity which brings great benefit to the self. No matter what the situation, it makes everything easy and light.

You have to look after your self-respect so carefully, making sure you never lose it. The basis for maintaining it is Humility.

IV   Protection

There is a great deal of power in humility.

Sometimes that power is useful for your own protection. Sometimes it is useful in the protection of others.

The power of humility allows you to see the benefit in everything, even in the insults of others.

It enables you to say, "Maybe there's something for me to learn here. Someone is saying this to me, there must be something to it."

Even insults become learning situations, naturally.

You don't feel a need to get upset. You aren't affected in a negative way.

Your own self-respect works to keep you steady, no matter what the criticism coming your way.

Even if the problem is theirs, not yours, and there's nothing for you to change in yourself, still, humility removes the need for you to say so.

Real humility results in so much power of truth and inner silence, that you don't need to say anything at all in words.

The very power of your inner state of being will make the other person realize the error of their ways.

Your only desire at that time is the hope that they will be touched by your humility, so that they can open and begin to enjoy their humility, too.

V Giving

Sometimes people are not open to being touched by humility. They do not yet understand its power, and so they take advantage of your attitude, thinking you are weak.

If this is the case, then the first thing to remember is that it is your duty to help people . . .

And in this, it is important to be tireless in your giving. So, on the one hand, never give up, never completely stop, because one day they will definitely understand, they will definitely take your help.

However, on the other hand, it is equally as important to assess how worthy they are of your donation.

Understanding the value of what you are giving is a first step; understanding the one to whom you are giving is the second.

If they have no value for what they are being given, it is as though what you are giving is going to waste.

You need wisdom to understand these two things: the value of what you are giving and the extent to which the other person is taking benefit.

If you are giving in full, but they are just throwing it aside, what is the point in giving to that degree? Humility does not mean to waste your resources. Humility means to have the wisdom to understand the power of your resources and give accordingly.

VI   Understanding

Some people feel that to have humility or to be humble involves bowing down and being subservient to others. They find it very difficult to cultivate their humility. This has not been my experience.

To me, humility means to understand the self, and through that, to understand others as well.

Thinking about humility is like thinking about an old friend— someone from whom you have learned a lot, someone who has taught you a great deal.

Developing humility has brought a lot of comfort and rest into my life.

VII   Love

Humility as a power is based on a very elevated awareness of who you are.

Such a high state of consciousness makes you very cool, very peaceful and very loving.

One with humility is full of both love and respect. Because they are full, their only desire is to give. One with humility is never selfish.

Humility makes the heart open and generous. There is never the desire to receive from others.

Humility makes it easy to have relationships of love and respect with everyone.

When there is humility, you enjoy understanding the hearts of others. You want to understand the hearts of others.

Humility allows you to accept what someone else is saying. (If you accept today what others are saying, then they will accept tomorrow whatever you say.)

One who has humility constantly remains happy and makes others happy, too. A person with humility will always say, "Whatever I am, whatever I've got, it's fine. I'm happy, I'm content."

A person with humility never gets angry. A person with humility is easygoing. If you have humility, people come close to you, with love. Humility emerges your divinity.

Part Two

I   The Enemy

Humility and arrogance are enemies.

Where there is arrogance, there cannot possibly be humility. And where there is humility, there cannot possibly be arrogance.

If you have dislike, hatred or jealousy for anyone, you can't have humility.

If you have the attitude of give me, give me, give me, or the feeling that no one should touch anything of yours, you will not be able to develop humility.

If you have the habit of pointing the finger at others, saying: "This one is doing this . . . this one is doing that . . . they should be doing this . . . they should be doing that," then you can't develop humility.

If you have the desire to receive respect from others, you can't be humble.

If you want position or possession, you can't be humble.

II   The Loss

Arrogance usually begins from external things, but it ends up deep inside the soul, penetrating everything, destroying it all.

Arrogance creates anger and greed.

Think about it.

A person with ego always has a lot of anger and greed. There is also a lot of stubbornness.

A person with ego says, "I'm not getting any respect." They say, "No one loves me."

One who has arrogance does not have any real love or mercy.

They do not have the power to understand the hearts of others. They do not want to understand the hearts of others.

A person with arrogance is distanced from others.

III   The Loss in Service

Arrogance will prevent you from serving people well. It finishes off whatever honesty there was in your service.

Your service to others becomes limited by selfish motives. You use it to inflate your limited sense of self. The sign of this is

Humility and Empowerment

the need to see the immediate reward of your effort. It is like eating unripe fruit. It makes you ill.

Arrogance makes you impatient.

IV Loss in Relationship

If your service is based on ego, you won't be able to take help from God.

Without God, you feel alone. Alone, you can't do anything.

It is as if you become artificial, because without God there's no inner strength at all.

V Renouncing Arrogance

By placing you on the same wavelength, humility allows you to develop a very good relationship with God, naturally.

Humility allows you to take love, peace and happiness from God.

These are drawn from Him automatically, when there is humility in your interaction with others.

Those with humility carry on in service without ever needing to see the fruits of their labor.

Humility teaches you how to renounce arrogance.

Part Three

Humility is the mother of all virtues.

Do you feel this? Think about it.

If you have every virtue except this one of humility, you will be a virtuous human being who is arrogant about your virtues.

However, as someone who is all virtuous, as well as humble, you will be an incarnation of the divine.

I   Humility as a Power

Real humility should never be confused with low self-esteem.

I'll share a very personal secret with you: Just as I would never seek to control anyone, neither will I ever allow anyone to control me.

Just as I would never force myself on anyone, neither will anyone ever be able to force themselves on me. These are not the words of arrogance.

On the contrary, they are the words of self-respect.

Real humility, that is, humility as a power, is another word for self-respect.

If your humility is real, then that humility will carry you, keep you on top of everything, as if humility were like wings, born of enthusiasm for your beautiful truth.

Humility teaches you the art of flying.

The destination might be very high, but with wings such as these, you will definitely succeed.

Another secret is that your ego is not going to go away just like that.

In fact, it is going to follow you everywhere! Even into meditations filled with great light . . .

You'll just be sitting there when all of a sudden, this or that thought from your limited self will emerge, pulling you down in a second.

To come down like that means you are still open to influences of a lesser order. This is a sign of ego.

Actually, any time you are negatively influenced, either by internal or external sources, the root cause of it is ego. Ego is very subtle, which is why it is not easily detected.

It works underground undermining your very foundation of truth.

Anything, everything, can end up inflating it: people's comments, criticisms, all sorts of circumstances and situations—anything can act as a trigger.

And you are taken over completely.

However, if you stay alert and pay attention to yourself, you will be able to maintain your humility regardless.

You will be able to remember that whatever is happening is a test.

You are being tested on your determination to not allow anything to touch your wings.

Be very careful about how you use your eyes and ears.

Talk to them. Tell your eyes, "This is how you must see!" and your ears, "This is not what you're going to listen to!"

Maintain your self-respect by remembering that you are not going to allow ego to reach you, you are going to keep it behind you . . .

While you just continue to fly.

II   The Humility of a Tree

The greatest virtue of all is humility.

This is because humility allows you to be virtuous with others, unconditionally.

See the humility of a fruit tree. When it is in season and its branches are full of fruit, see how they bend and bow, making it easy for others to take what they have to offer.

Similarly, when your character is full of virtue, then your willingness to bow and bend makes it easy for others to take all you have to offer.

A tree whose branches start high up will not be able to bend and bow very much. For this reason, it is difficult to take its fruits.

Ego is like that.

You may be holding your head up very high, but in fact, you are not offering anything of much value to anyone.

Just think about it. What would a life filled with humility be like? And what is it like without it?

III   God's Example

God is the Highest on High. Yet God is completely humble.

Even though He is the One who does everything, He hides Himself away, saying, "I don't do anything."

No matter how high we reach, we, too, must always be humble.

IV   Cultivating Humility

In order to develop the humility of self-respect, you need to understand yourself deeply and clearly.

You need to understand the power of your own truth, and then develop your character on the basis of that.

The humility of self-respect comes from knowing what you were, originally, and are, eternally.

In other words, it means to know yourself as a child of God.

For this, internal honesty to your highest self and to God, is very important.

So is patience.

Also, always think of yourself as a continual learner.

Never think that you have found everything, done everything, know everything.

Never entertain negative feelings or biased ideas about people. Keep your heart very open and clean, because humility needs a good home to dwell in.

At the deepest layers of your being, pure currents of your original state still exist.

These currents are free from ego.

The more your meditation takes you into soul consciousness, the more you will experience this ego-free you.

To experience this is to know you are coming close to God.

V   Conclusion

Humility teaches us the art of life.

By teaching us how to maintain our self-respect, and to give respect to others, humility makes life so beautiful.

It is through humility that the heart opens to the most beautiful truth:

We have a right to God's love.

Part B

Living the Vision
Questions and Responses

1

SPIRITUALITY IN EVERYDAY LIFE

Is there really a perfect self?
How is it achieved?

Let's start by imagining a diamond. In order to get a diamond to sparkle, the first thing you have to do is clean it.

The same principle applies to us.

Originally, the soul was like a pure diamond.

In order to restore that original sparkle, the debris that has accumulated on the soul first has to be removed.

Debris means the mistakes we have made. These sit in the soul like flaws in a diamond.

Perfection is about removing the flaws in the soul.

However, there is more to it than that.

Beyond removing the falsehood from the soul, perfection is really about inculcating Truth.

It is Truth that makes the soul sparkle.

I   Truth

Truth is purity in reality.

What do we mean by purity? Purity means being honest to your highest self.

It means developing such deep honesty that God Himself is attracted and that attraction becomes visible through you.

Truth means purity to this degree, in everyday life.

Your whole way of being becomes based on this ultimate degree of honesty—to your self, God and others.

This kind of honesty—complete, absolute and of the highest order—is real, and it makes you real, too.

This is a very important aspect because it is only honesty to this degree that removes the mistakes, or flaws, from the soul.

II   The Hearts of Others

Another aspect of perfection is the effect of your mistakes on others. This has to be removed.

It is one thing to be honest with the self and God, to acknowledge your mistakes on both levels and to feel good about having been honest from within . . .

But it is another thing to remove your mistakes from the hearts of others. That takes a lot of honesty! Even more than it takes to be honest with your own self or God. Why? Because often people are less afraid of God than they are of what other people might say or think.

Nonetheless, it is not hard to remove your mistakes from the hearts of others. You can do it in one sitting.

Simply see their heart, let your own heart be melted, and give them the company of your Truth.

This is the way to become a pure diamond; that is, to emerge your perfect self.

〜

What keeps me from fulfilling my highest potential?

There are three kinds of circumstances which will keep you from living up to your highest potential.

One is to allow yourself to be influenced by others. The second is to allow yourself to be controlled. The third is to have attachment to anyone or anything.

It is good to check yourself to see if any of these circumstances are operating in your life and, if they are, to what degree.

I Influences

The danger in being open to the haphazard influence of those around you is threefold. Firstly, it will ultimately keep you from experiencing the influence of God.

Secondly, it will prevent you from being able to recognize and experience your own true self. Thirdly, the total effect of these first two factors will make it difficult for you to come close to God.

It is also important to note that these influences are not just restricted to those external to you; they can also come from within.

Arrogance is an example of this, as are any programmings and conditionings that come from the lower self.

II   Being Controlled

Allowing yourself to be controlled can lead you to be so cut off from the experience of your own uniqueness and specialties, that you are barely able to stand up even for your own self.

This kind of "controlling" doesn't have to be the result of external forces alone.

Many people exert this kind of repression on their own kinder nature, talents and/or inner conscience.

Anger is an example of this. To be controlled by your own anger is to repress your original qualities of tolerance and love.

Allowing yourself to be controlled, either by others or by your own self, over a long period of time creates a very deep kind of sorrow in the soul.

The way to free yourself from unwanted influences and from being controlled is to understand that you are not just the child of God, but that you are also His heir.

What this means is that everything He has is also yours.

God always says, "Children you are the masters. . . . Everything of Mine is yours . . ."

Appreciate that God does not seek to control anyone.

You need only to recognize God and your own true self, and then come close to both.

This puts you back in charge.

III   Attachment

Attachment means being dependent, either on someone or something, for your state of well-being.

It is the result of identifying yourself too strongly with external things, like position, possessions and other people.

(A healthier state would be to identify with the more subtle truths within you, such as the divinity and dignity of being God's child.)

Another way of saying this is that attachment makes you dependent, like an invalid on crutches, on one or another external support.

Of the three blocks to being able to live out your highest truth, attachment is the worst. It creates a huge amount of loss.

Whereas influence colors your personality, and controlling obscures parts of your personality, attachment destroys personality altogether.

This is because of the way it makes you dependent on other people and things, to the point of never fully cultivating your own personality, yourself.

Attachment deceives you into thinking that you don't need to develop your truth to its fullest potential.

You think that life on what is the equivalent of emotional crutches is a good life. Also, you falsely imagine that those crutches will last you forever.

Unlike influences or controlling, attachment is a self-willed, self-imposed limiting of the self.

Because the experience of being influenced or controlled is usually quite painful, people generally end up seeking ways to rid themselves of it.

However, in the case of attachment, the damage is more subtle. People are less aware of it and, therefore, do not readily engage themselves in becoming free.

IV The Loss

Attachment keeps you from developing the all-embracing exhilaration of self and God-realization—the constant experience of being a child of God, part of God's family, the light of God's eyes.

With attachment, you will not be able to experience the power of God's love and blessings, nor enjoy His unbroken companionship.

The result of this is that it will be very difficult to rise above the defects and impurities in the soul, to claim the inheritance of divinity to which you are entitled.

Constant, natural happiness will continually elude you. It doesn't even matter what the attachment is: to your own image of yourself, to the image you have of others, to the specialties of others, a certain style . . .

Attachment destroys you—the real you—completely.

V   Solutions

To free yourself of all three of these states of bondage, continue to increase the quality of your thinking and of your general state of mind.

Keep moving forward! Cultivate the feeling that no one and nothing can stop you.

Understand each one is playing a role and play your part accordingly.

Never go into questions about *why*, as in "Why is this person always doing this?", or *what*, as in "What is this person up to now?"

These questions will distance you from others and keep others distant from you.

Avoid the thought that others should do what you tell them to do. Learn to develop the loving feeling that everyone should do only what God wants us to do.

Think about these things and you will see how much inner transformation there can be.

Your eyes will open and you'll be able to recognize your own (true) self and also God.

This is what sets you free.

～

How can I remain free from tension?

First of all, make sure that your breath, thoughts and time are being used in a worthwhile way. There is power in using these three things well.

This power also invokes the company of the Almighty Authority. And this creates even more power.

This is useful because to manage the energies of life nowadays, you do need a lot of power.

The method for this is to become an accurate companion of God in His task, at every moment, with your every thought and every breath.

I   Thoughts

In the case of thought, it is a matter of making each thought useful. A useful thought is one that brings benefit to yourself and to others.

For example: thoughts which serve to increase the experience of your own value and help you to realize the value of your life are useful thoughts.

II Breath

What is meant by breath is your whole way of being. For example, it is actually quite possible to give lecture after lecture, without ever feeling tired or even having any feelings of discomfort.

How? Because of the way you give the speech; that is, how you use your energy.

Using energy in the right way means not to become emotional, not to get overexcited, but rather to always remain calm and collected.

"Rushing" your breath even slightly while carrying out a task, will definitely create a loss of power and feelings of distress.

III Time

The above points will enable you to master your relationship with time. In fact, time will automatically be used successfully if breath and thought are used well.

Think about these powerful factors and experiment with them practically. You will see how they help you to manage the stress in your everyday life.

Is it really possible to forgive and forget?

Yes it is, but it needs to happen the other way around. First you have to forget. Then your forgiveness can be real.

You will never really be able to forgive an incident or situation, if your heart or head is still holding on to it.

You have to be able to let it go.

You have to really be able to forget the scene, to such an extent that it's as if nothing even happened and you know nothing about it at all.

I   Remembering

The way to achieve this level of "forgetting," however, is less a matter of forgetting and more a matter of remembering . . .

We need to be remembering something else entirely; namely, the significance of that incident in our life, now.

This is the effort to make when a scene you wish to forget comes in front of you. Say to it, again and again, "Okay, but what does this have to do with me, here and now?"

II   Our Duty

In fact I don't even like to use this word "forget." The process of trying to forget something in itself will keep reminding you of what you want to forget.

Why should you want to do that to yourself?

There are so many things it is our duty to remember, like our own dignity and divinity, not to mention that of others. "Forgetting" is not the problem. "Forgetting" is not our duty.

Remembering is.

How do I forgive my own self?

Self-forgiveness takes place on two different levels. The first level is practical and straightforward.

The second requires a very subtle and secret kind of effort, which is worthwhile understanding, because the process is extraordinary and far more permanent.

I The Practical Effort

On the first level of effort, the first step is to realize that you have made a mistake. It is not a case—as it is in forgiving others—of simply forgetting the mistake! To think that you can simply forget your mistakes and everything will be okay is to be careless.

Instead, there needs to be realization about the seriousness of your mistake.

No matter how small other people may consider them to be, it is good to consider even your smallest mistakes to be big ones.

The true dignity and reality of the self does not allow for anything less.

II Signs

If you have honestly realized your mistake, but your mind continues to go over and over it, to no avail, consider this a sign that you are now in need of forgiving yourself.

Another sign is when, having realized the mistake, the soul is flooded with feelings of guilt, accompanied by an unstoppable flow of unnecessary thoughts.

Why feel guilty?

Learning how to forgive yourself is a much better use of your time.

Finally, be careful about remaining too much on your own.

This can emerge a lot of old, internal patterns and thoughts will again begin to circle uselessly over and over in your mind.

III Spiritual Awareness

With these signs alerting you to the need for self-forgiveness, the next step is to understand what to do.

On the first, practical level of self-forgiveness, it is a question of using your spiritual training to discover new ways of looking at the situation.

Injecting your spirituality into a mistake creates freshness. You get a new hold on the present, which enables you to let go of the past.

There is new enthusiasm for doing things the right way.

The thought is, "Okay, it's over now. Let me move on."

This produces hope for the soul and renewed feelings of interest for the task of self-transformation.

IV   Doing It Right

If feelings of guilt are the problem, what you need to do is engage yourself in better things.

After realizing your mistake, there is no need to go on punishing yourself.

Involving yourself instead in good actions will not only erase a mistake, it will also replace it with a higher, more honest, inner programming.

It's just like recording an audiocassette.

If you've taped something poorly, and the recording isn't good, you wouldn't spend a lot of time crying about it. You would simply record over the mistake.

In the same way, instead of losing sleep over whatever wrong you have done, get busy instead in doing something right.

This is what allows you to put the past to rest, once and for all.

V   Positive Influences

If a lot of old things are coming up and there is a flow of
unwanted thoughts from the past, the next step is to put
yourself under some positive influences.

Put yourself into good company!

The company of those who exude the vibration of peace can
be a very effective influence. Have at least this much mercy
on your self . . .

VI   The Subtle Effort

On the second, more subtle level of self-forgiveness, the effort
is more internal. At this level, mistakes are addressed from
within.

If the mistake involves words or actions and you find that the
mistake keeps repeating itself—in other words, there has been
no transformation— then you can understand that you have
not yet done the truly internal work of taking care of the
problem at the level of its roots.

You might defend yourself, saying, "This is just the way I am,
this is my usual tone of voice, this is how I always act, etc."

However, the truth is that this mistake has now become your
habit . . . it is now a part of the way you speak and behave.

You will find that even if you want to change it, you can't.

VII   Change of Attitude

What needs to happen in order to erase even the last traces of a mistake is nothing less than a total change of attitude.

Until your attitude toward that mistake changes, it will continue to come up again and again, coloring your thoughts, speech, behavior . . . everything.

VIII   Checking Yourself

What you need to do is cultivate the habit of checking yourself on a very deep level. Go deeply into that introspective state of remembrance, where the dignity of your original divinity lies.

Check yourself against this highest, innermost truth.

This is a very subtle kind of checking, which by itself does all the work.

IX   Real Change

This is a very wonderful secret; note it well! To start thinking, "Well, now, I have to forget and now I have to forgive," etc. is a very complicated and time-consuming process. It is not even very effective!

However, by using the more subtle method of measuring yourself against your highest truth and letting the power of self-realization work for you, you will find that your role in life will change.

The role of being one who makes mistakes will end.

And you will actually see, coming toward you, the role of being your perfect self.

You will start moving toward that more stable state.

It is the moment when your original, divine characteristics, such as purity, peace, love and joy, again start working for you more and more.

These personality traits of divinity deep within are an enormous help in the process of transformation.

Emerge them! Use them! They automatically work to remove all those other, useless traits.

And what you thought was impossible becomes possible.

Your process of transformation becomes real and you start changing. Truly.

How can I protect myself from the negativity of others?

It is not difficult to protect yourself from the negative tendencies of others.

Regular yoga practice—one which thoroughly immerses you in your spiritual identity—will ultimately allow you to disassociate from such negativity completely.

I   The Spiritual Buffer

It works like this: A good experience of your spiritual identity puts you back in touch with your inner peace.

The more this is experienced—and given expression—the stronger it gets, until ultimately it becomes like a buffer against the negative reactions you would have otherwise.

This ability to disassociate from the negativity around you and inside you is known as the power of detachment.

It is the basis of being able to remain true to your own values regardless of the moods of others.

It is also the basis for creating an atmosphere filled with your own peace and love, which in itself is a most wonderful form of spiritual service.

II   Serving Through Vibrations

Souls are definitely served through your vibrations of peace and love, so never stop giving this form of support in your interactions with others.

The subtle art of serving through your vibrations is the basis for receiving the subtle love and help coming to you from God.

If you stop this kind of service, you will also stop that flow to you from God.

How dry and empty the heart feels, when the subtle link with the Supreme is broken in this way.

III   Patience

Actually, it is only when you allow yourself to become depleted in this way that you then become vulnerable to the moods of other people.

How else could another person's vibrations have more of an effect on you than God's vibrations? Keep yourself strong by proceeding with faith and patience.

Eventually, all will come to realize the help that is coming to them, through you.

How do I increase my emotional stability?

First of all, let's understand what emotions are.

Emotions are a more surfaced expression of feelings. Feelings are deeper.

Whatever is the quality of your feelings, so will be the quality of your emotions.

At the core of your innermost being are innately pure feelings like love and peace. The more you activate these within yourself, the less your habitual emotions of negativity can come into play.

The easy way to activate these innate feelings of quality is to understand and explore your spiritual identity.

I   Introspection

A good way to begin exploring your spiritual identity is to develop the virtue of introspection.

Introspection means having the desire to become good, and involving yourself in efforts which will make that happen.

(Extroversion means having the desire to have others think you are good, and involving yourself in the efforts which will make that happen.)

Introspection will ultimately allow you to see your true self in the mirror of your heart.

II   The Spiritual Identity

To bring yourself into a state of anger, depression or general confusion requires only the old habit of thinking too much.

Bringing yourself into a state of inner stability and calm requires something different—like courage and peace.

It is also good to have a lot of love for God.

Yet, to understand the self, have a good relationship with God and be able to enjoy good communication with others is actually easy.

Simply keep touching base with that core of pure feelings—your divinity—which is the foundation of your spiritual identity. This cools the brain and keeps the heart very clean and honest.

It is not necessary to get into all sorts of things inside your head. On the contrary, a level head and an honest heart are all that are needed.

No longer ruled by roller-coaster emotions, your true nature of divinity will ultimately begin to assert itself. It will begin to exert its own influence.

And you, the real you, will be freed.

How can I know when love is real?
When can I trust love?

To begin with, let's be sure we understand this word "trust."

Trust is made up of many other qualities, like love and respect. For example, if you feel that someone truly respects you, then you are more inclined to trust their love.

Also, trust is something of the heart, more than of the head. It is the result of a feeling you get from others, from their attitude and/or vibrations.

I The Real Question

However, the real question about love is not about trusting others, but rather, how much can others trust the love coming from you?

To what degree have you earned the trust of others?

This is important because there is a lot of power in becoming worthy of another's trust. If you have this power, you won't need to worry if the love coming your way is true or not.

This power transforms all love—however artificial or false it may be—into something lovely, pure and true.

Actually, this is how God's love works on us.

We had only human, superficial love. Yet His pure love is transforming that, filling our hearts and transforming our desires.

II   Earning Trust

To earn the trust of others, you need to become completely clean inside. This means becoming completely selfless and honest.

The love of a clean heart is unconditional.

It doesn't require anything in return for what it gives. It just flows automatically, like waterfalls do after rain.

In such a state, "giving" is not done to anyone as a favor, but simply as a way of being, or a way of taking care of yourself.

There's never any feeling of having given too much, of not having received the return of your love or of not having been appreciated.

III   God's Love

When you are clean inside, it is easy to take God's love. This love is not a question of anything physical.

It is a subtle experience received through your spiritual, incorporeal state.

Because it is a real, pure vibration of love, you trust it automatically.

No one should ever have to instill in you faith in God's love. You trust it on the basis of your own experience.

IV   Barriers to Love

Whatever is in your heart that is not clean, not true, will ultimately begin to act like a wall, obstructing the natural flow of love.

People who say that there is no love in their life, are being blocked by this wall.

Actually, there is love, but they just can't accept it.

Ego is the clearest example of this.

Ego limits the flow of love by placing conditions on the love you give and receive.

Ego uses love to satisfy its own needs and desires. It produces a love which is deceptive, one which brings only temporary satisfaction.

Ego does not allow you to experience true love or share it.

Spirituality in Everyday Life

God

In fact, ego is capable of destroying your ability to feel love altogether.

V Real Love

The problem nowadays is that love is interpreted on a gross level. Just as many people are attracted to the size and glitter of a fake diamond, so are they swayed by false, superficial love. There is no value in either.

A real diamond is often quite small, but it is flawless. That is where its value lies.

Real love is like a tiny diamond: it is not flashy and it is without a single flaw.

Real love is one hundred percent pure. There is nothing artificial mixed into it.

It is clean.

There are no ulterior motives in real love.

VI More About Real Love

When I was young, I used to love watching waterfalls. It would start raining and water would start flowing.

When rain hits the ground, it becomes muddy, but while it is still in the waterfall, it stays completely clean.

You can even drink it, it is so pure. No one, nothing, has touched that water.

It is like that with pure love.

The more you awaken Truth in you, the more you will be able to recognize—and take in—the pure love coming to you from God like clear water.

As you fill yourself with this pure, spiritual love, others will be able to see it.

And they will trust it too, feeling it to be true.

〜

How can I maintain good relationships with others?

To start with, avoid thinking that you cannot get along with someone because of their personality.

Humility and the genuine feeling of wanting to learn from others are very effective in creating harmony.
(As opposed to thinking that you are here to teach them!)

The more spirituality there is in your relationships, the easier it is to have good interactions, constantly.

An awareness of your own spiritual identity fills your character with beauty and spirituality. This becomes a basis for good moods, good feelings about yourself, and even for a good atmosphere and vibration around you.

I Self-Respect

Self-respect is essential for good relationships.

It is developed by cultivating a spiritual awareness of yourself and raising your thinking to the level where it can tune in to God.

It is easy to remain in a state of self-respect when you spend a lot of time like this, up above, with God.

Self-respect is not developed by coming down, again and again, from your divine state of inner dignity, in reaction to negative forces (external or internal).

Be very cautious of being affected, or influenced, by anything. If you are so affected, repeatedly, it means that there is some weakness in you.

It means that you are still looking to be supported by something external to the self.

This is not an aspect of self-respect. It is not true to your inherent dignity.

The inherent dignity of each, based on self-sovereignty, is the true foundation of harmony in relationships.

II Harmonizing Personalities

Harmonizing our personalities is the greatest challenge we face.

Three qualities which allow us to best rise to this challenge are love, mercy and forgiveness.

First and foremost to our own self.

Be merciful and forgive your own self . . . and with love, forget the things of the past and move forward.

Then you will be able to have real feelings of mercy and love for others.

This is the way to truly be of help to others.

III   Helping Others

True help does not mean empathizing with the suffering of others to such an extent that you lose your own happiness.

Be careful of this.

Our duty is to maintain a healthy inner state of being constantly, so that no matter what the state of those around us, our influence is the stronger one bringing them into happiness, too.

IV   God's Help

It takes courage to remain forgiving, loving and merciful.

Simply by being clear that this is your responsibility, invokes the help of God.

Then because God, the One who is called the Remover of Sorrow, is with you the sorrow of others is easily removed.

The Bestower of Peace and Happiness is your Father.

It is His power which removes the sorrow and bestows the happiness. These qualities of His will reach others through you.

This is the continuous effort of one with a true heart. It makes you a true instrument in God's task.

How do I remain honest in relationships?

First of all, let's understand what honesty in relationships looks like.

It looks like love.

So don't ever stop giving love. Anything else is dishonest.

Honesty means to not give up on a relationship; it means to not break apart simply because of personality clashes.

To resolve problems by giving up or going away is to deceive yourself. The same difficulty will occur either with someone else or in another situation.

The most elevated effort for remaining honest in relationships is to transform whatever weaknesses are in you. This is an art which can be learned by anyone.

You only need to want to!

2

GOD

What is the personality of God?

I would like to share with you my experience of God as a very extraordinary, very loving, totally unique personality.

I say unique because there is no human being who can have a personality like God's, no matter how learned or saintly he or she may be.

No one can know and follow, to the extent that God does, all the laws of the universe, and yet be so completely loving.

No one is capable of as much mercy, forgiveness and love.

No one can understand, as does God, the difficulties in which we humans find ourselves in today's world.

And there is no one who can protect us from them like He does, either.

I   The Light of God

In some faith traditions, it is said that God is as bright as a thousand suns. Importance is given to the brightness of that light. Some interpretations would even have you fear its intensity.

However, it is not that God's light would literally be so frightening. It is just that it is so unique, you are completely awed by it.

There is so much power in the rays of that light . . . enough, actually, to destroy all the negativity on this planet.

Only this beautiful light of God's can dispel our own darkness in such a way.

II   Enlightenment

What, in fact, does it really mean to say that God is light?

It means that the recognition of God brings light . . . as in "enlightenment."

It means that in the recognition of God is the recognition of your own highest self.

It means that the more you come to know God, the more the negativity in the soul can be removed. This is another aspect of God's utter uniqueness. No matter how degenerated we may have become, God's love and light uplift us from that state.

We need only raise our eyes and look to Him.

III That Which Is Eternal

When people look at other people, they see their external appearance: how they are dressed, the way they look and so on. However, one should not see the outer, physical appearance.

My eyes see the soul, the spiritual being.

The physical body is perishable, as are all relationships among human beings. These are not going to remain with you forever.

So the training I have given to my eyes from early on has been to search for the One who is eternal.

When there is that deep desire to experience that which is eternal, then, even though the eyes continue to take in all that is physical, they are no longer distracted.

The ears hear what's going on in the world but they are no longer drawn in or affected.

You need to be able to move your intellect away from all external distractions and instead center it exclusively on God.

Then you will be able to see that Light.

And that Light will enter your life.

What is Dadi's experience of God's love?

My deepest desire for everyone is that they come to know the love of God.

Once or twice in meditation I have had the wonderful experience of seeing God's heart.

God's heart is so huge, so generous! Anyone reaching it seems to simply be dissolved in it.

Truly it is wide open, just waiting for us to come.

I   God as Mother

Someone once asked me if thinking about God as the Mother is all right.

With all my heart this is one experience I would like to share.

God is definitely our Mother.

In fact, God is first of all our Mother, and only then our Father.

This experience brings so much happiness.

When we know God as our Mother there are so many feelings of acceptance.

Our mistakes are dispelled—with love.

No questions need even be asked . . .

II Love

Who can be absorbed by God's heart? Only those who have a heart like God's: no untruths, no negativity . . .

For these souls, God has so much love. It's as if they get tucked away in special corners of His heart.

God is very attached to us, you know. He teaches us to free ourselves from attachments, but He has got a lot of attachment to us.

There is so much love coming to us from God. By comparison, physical mothers and fathers don't know how to love their children at all . . .

III Canopy of Protection

I feel so well looked after by God, that my only desire at this point is that everyone should have this experience, too.

God's love frees you from all worries and concerns. After all, whatever could there be to worry about when it is God who is looking after you?

So my pure desire for all is that you should experience this love, and these kinds of feelings because many of you are so innocent and vulnerable.

You give up so quickly!

Did you know that God has a very special and beautiful umbrella, open and ready for all the children? What is this umbrella? It is His canopy of protection.

To sit in God's heart means to be under this canopy.

My deepest desire is that everyone should experience God's beautiful heart in this way.

The canopy of God's protection is this love.

↬

What is the role of faith?

When I decided to devote my life to God and took up the appropriate lifestyle for this, people laughed at me.

Women were simply not allowed to do such things, in the India of those days.

So people laughed, saying, "We'll see how she will manage. We will see how long she lasts. She must be crazy . . ."

I was nineteen years old then, and I remember saying "God, no matter what happens to me, I am going to be your true and proper child."

"Even if the entire world is on one side and I am alone on the other, I am going to be Yours."

And I could feel God's response, "She has nobody. So she has Me."

To which I said, "Yes. I have no one. Except You."

I Faith

My experience is that sweet conversations like this keep God very close to you. Even though God is very elevated, and His qualities and virtues are the highest of all, still, you are His child.

You are His child; He is your Parent. You belong to each other.

Shouldn't it therefore be possible for you to know Him as He really is?

II Knowing

Previously, while praying to God, I used to say, "Okay, God, this is it. Now tell me. Are You going to come to me? Or am I going to come to You?"

I'd be very stubborn about it!

I also used to feel that I would recognize Him the moment He came. I felt sure I would know when it was Him.

I imagined that some ancient part of me would start speaking, saying, "Yes. Now I have found what I was looking for . . ."

When at last that day did come, the day I had been waiting for so long, this was exactly the experience I had.

It was exactly this sound and feeling that emerged from deep within.

III   The Path We Share

The voice of faith is so necessary in this.

If you maintain your faith, while managing all your other duties, you hasten that moment when God reveals Himself to you.

If the pulse of your desire is intense, God can come to you right here and now. I know from my own experience that that moment arrives because of the deep longing to experience God.

It is not even a matter of who has come to whom. It's just the absoluteness of the experience.

For whatever the differences among our traditions, I know that the one thing within us all is the deep, inner yearning to experience God.

This deep desire, in itself, is the way to God. This is the path we all share.

IV   It Is the Same

The one thing missing from the lives of us all is the same.

The sorrow and happiness of all, no matter what the caste, creed or color is the same.

What we are all searching for is, therefore, the same.

V Fruits of Our Labor

At a certain point in our search, after all the scriptures have been studied, and still there has not been any personal meeting with God, finally, we turn to God and say,

"Okay, God. Now You have to reveal Yourself to me. *You* show *me* Your path."

And God says, "Forget everything you know of this world."

And then the sweet fruit of all your searching and all your faith begins to emerge. The search comes to an end. So does the desperation.

And we say, "Thank you, God. This is what I wanted. I wanted nothing else . . .

Except that in my eyes should be Your light

And that this light show others the path to You, too . . ."

How can the mind be linked to God?

To begin with, understand that the mind is not the only faculty of the soul.

Another faculty is the "buddhi" which, roughly translated, can be called the intellect—not the intellect of intellectual study, but rather the part of you that is capable of knowing right from wrong.

I Yoga

It is the intellect which is responsible for forming the link with God. However, it will not be able to do so if the mind does not let it.

In other words, the mind has to become peaceful and cooperative first.

For the soul to be linked to God, the intellect and the mind have to work together.

Only when there is this kind of harmony between the two can there then be that link with God.

Actually, this is what we call yoga.

II Difficulties

One reason it is sometimes difficult to have this yoga (or union with God), is because the intellect, through weakness or laziness, just won't make the effort to create that link.

At other moments, it may be the intellect which desires to make that connection.

However, the mind gets into so much mischief—thinking and worrying about so many things—that the intellect isn't able to be still enough to allow that link to happen.

III   The Solution

The solution is to focus on the intellect.

This is because the intellect, when strong and healthy, actually acts like a mother to the mind. It is capable of keeping it nicely under control.

The intellect is made strong and healthy through a continual supply of proper spiritual study. This is what makes it divine.

A mature, divine intellect will always be able to keep the mind—the child—under control.

In fact, a healthy intellect can even command the mind to turn itself toward God.

As the mind and intellect learn to work together, the connection with God can be made very easily.

What is the influence of God on our thoughts?

There is a lot of light coming to us from God; a light which is not of a physical nature.

It is spiritual light, as in "enlightenment."

It touches our intellect, opening a lock on our awareness. And we find ourselves again receptive to all of God's powers—like love and peace.

These again start filling the soul. And the feeling is of having found something precious that we had somehow lost.

I Understanding

So much understanding and love is restored to the soul through this Godly influence on the intellect. It is as if a door to understanding opens up completely.

Surely, this is where He gets His title "Intellect of the Wise," as is mentioned in some of the world's scriptures.

II Discovery

Can you appreciate the difference in states of mind before and after this light touches your being?

Love had become so difficult.

There are difficulties with love on all levels—for the self and in relation to others.

And then His love reached us, making the soul blossom.

And we begin to realize how much we had missed this love.

The feeling is: "I've found what I've been looking for . . . . . . the One to whom I belong, eternally."

Our thinking totally changes. And so do we.

What is Dadi's experience of the meeting with God?

Normally when a person dies, friends and relatives feel that the one they loved has gone, and the body has just been left behind.

In the experience of being with God, the soul does not actually leave the body, but the feeling, nevertheless, is of having left everything behind.

The feeling is that the body is here, this world is here, but I am sitting with God and God alone.

Nothing distracts you. You are just with God. That is all.

You are in the body, but you are not trapped by it.

This is another way of saying that you are no longer tied down by superficial needs and supports.

You feel free. And you are.

3

THE WORLD

What is Dadi's vision of peace for the world?

In the days when we were designing our International Office in London, the architect said to me, "What do you want this to look like? A temple? A church? A mosque?"

I told him, "None of those."

"I want it to look like a home. For everyone."

I told him that we wanted something that wouldn't feel as if it belonged to any one religion in particular; but rather, that it belonged to everyone.

We wanted everyone who came to feel they were at home.

I The Challenge

Having traveled across the world I have seen that the deep desire in human hearts is for there to be oneness.

The people of the world want unity.

But how can this come about? How is it possible to have unity in a world where, even within families, let alone local communities, it is so lacking?

It is as if everyone has their own way of thinking. The ideas of others are not tolerated. Everyone wants to do everything their own way. Unity seems an unattainable ideal.

II   The Power of Truth

My experience, however, is that it is very easy to create unity and make others part of that unity, too.

We need only pay attention to one aspect, and that is to accumulate the power of truth.

This is because the power of truth alone can destroy the number one enemy of unity, which is ego.

When ego is out of the way, it is very easy to create an atmosphere of harmony.

This is the greatness of truth: the ability to come together with love, and accept each other's different ideas with love.

III   Cooperation

Each one of our five fingers is different. They are each unique, and yet it is only when the five fingers work together that whatever we put our hand to becomes successful.

Each finger has its own special capability, but the combination of specialties together creates a greater force.

If even one finger were missing, the task could not be accomplished with the same ease.

So each finger is unique, with its own special task. Yet success is the result of the harmony and cooperation between them all.

IV   God's Help

Go into the depths of truth. Understand what truth is. When the heart is filled with truth, everything else is removed from it.

Then there is no need for criticism. No need to compete in an unhealthy way. There are only clean, good feelings for all.

When we see the specialties of others and come together with a vision of unity and cooperation, God is also pleased.

"The Lord is pleased with a heart that is true." This is a saying in India, and it is true. God doesn't want anything else from us. All He wants is our true heart.

If the Lord is pleased, success is guaranteed.

The desire in everyone's heart is for the task of world transformation to be successful.

When our true hearts are presented in front of God, He will definitely work through us and all will be accomplished.

How can I overcome feelings of hopelessness?

Nowadays people say that there is nothing but corruption and evil in the world. But how did we reach this state?

And who will set it right if not we humans?

To truly contribute to the process of setting the world right, you need to develop a lot of inner, personal power.

This is because the path of someone who is trying to do something for the world will always be strewn with obstacles.

Not only can there be a complete lack of support for what you are trying to do, but there may even be many who will try to stop you.

Often it will be only your faith, courage and honesty that will enable you to carry on.

I   Faith

By faith I mean the faith that your task cannot fail, if you always remain honest in all of your dealings.

Faith, too, that your honesty and strength of conviction is the kind of courage that attracts the help of God.

In this way, you will never be alone and are sure to receive the support that you need.

II   A Strong Heart

Also, you need to make your heart strong. Make it
unbreakable!

This requires wisdom, such as the courage to never get
disheartened, and also the ability to tolerate everything.

Both of these qualities will keep you from feeling hurt . . .
especially the pain of feeling unappreciated when proper
recognition for your efforts or contribution is not forthcoming.

It is important to protect yourself from this because hurt feelings
create a lot of sadness, and sadness of any sort will undermine
the inner power already accumulated.

Before you know it, all your joy and enthusiasm will have
disappeared.

A strong heart that knows how to be wise enables you to
manage everything easily.

Always remember that the basis for complete success is an
honest, generous and clean heart.

Does Dadi have any advice for us?

When you look at the world through your physical eyes, you will see all the facets of our diversity: culture, race, personality, religion and so on.

Seeing only through your physical eyes, it is easy to become stubborn and to try to prove yourself right. However, where there is stubbornness, there is no love. And trying to prove the self right is equally offensive.

A diamond will sparkle even in the dust; you do not ever need to prove that you are right.

In the face of the dangers that come from seeing only with the physical eyes, I always think: Now is the time to go beyond all divisions, beyond all that limits us and our sense of self.

Whatever the race, the religion, the class—our consciousness now has to go beyond all of that.

I   Trustworthy and Honest in God's Task

Just as my concern is to be obedient to God and to be honest in God's work, so my advice to each one is to let there be obedience to God.

Whichever religion you belong to, whichever tradition you follow, let there just be that sense of obedience and the desire to be trustworthy and honest in God's task.

The One who is the most Beloved of all is the One who is standing in front of us with arms wide open, saying, "Break down the barriers . . . build bridges."

Whenever there is a barrier, people move back. They stop. But if there is a bridge, they go across. They move forward.

So cut down the barriers. And become those who are never stopped.

This is my experience of over sixty years. Neither can we stop anyone, nor can we be stopped, because this is the work of truth.

With the help of the Supreme Parent, it will be accomplished.

What no political, religious or scientific leader has been able to accomplish, will definitely be attained now . . .

Our collective power in this is the solution, in front of which nothing can be difficult.

II   The Power of Awareness

So often I hear people say, "This is difficult." However, I say: remove this word "difficult" from your vocabulary.

It is possible for human beings to do whatever they want. In fact, it is easy.

It is we humans who have created the world as it is today and so it is in our human hands to see it changed.

It all depends on our awareness. It all depends on our hearts.

Everyone's heart desires a better world. It is only a question of understanding how to make it happen.

III   The Inner State of Dignity

Sound judgment about what is right and what you need to do is based on your system of values.

It is only when you are standing on the foundation of your values that you are able to maintain your truth, no matter what the surrounding circumstances.

The ability to live according to your values, in an unwavering way, depends on how well you have realized your true spiritual identity, and have begun to cultivate that inner state of dignity.

This is the basis of spiritual power and it is this power which is most needed in the world today.

Every human being is currently in need of spiritual power. And only God can give it.

Spiritual power from God will come to you as you review and practice these concepts daily:

. . . the awareness of being God's child—which allows you to claim your divinity;

. . . the awareness of being a student—in which you need to be learning not just from God, but from those around you as well;

. . . the consciousness of being an example—that is, becoming the model of whatever you want others to learn;

. . . and the consciousness of being God's instrument—which means to use His qualities in every moment of your life.

This is the guaranteed method to fill yourself, as an individual, with strength . . . the spiritual strength coming to you from God.

This is what will allow you to understand your highest truth and begin to live it, easily.

In this way, the necessary degree of spiritual might and light created through the power of the gathering will definitely be attained.

4

MEDITATION

What is the "third eye"?

The concept of the third eye really refers to two quite common words. These two words are "I" and "mine."

There is so much wisdom in just these two words, if you know how to experience them in a deep way.

I Soul Consciousness

As a first step, imagine what it would be like to experience your Self in its highest form—the soul, in its original, pure state.

It is definitely possible to create such an experience. Indeed, this is what meditation is all about.

Meditation shifts you from one consciousness to another . . . from the limited, worldly one, called "body consciousness," to a more expanded, spiritual one, known as "soul consciousness."

Essentially, body consciousness is a state of having forgotten what your inner core of divinity is.

In soul consciousness, the soul feels distinct from the body. It is in it, but not of it.

Also, the soul feels completely separate from any negativity accumulated within it while being in a state of body consciousness over a long period of time.

To be in soul consciousness means to be in the experience of your original state of divinity. The soul feels light . . . enlightened . . . free!

In this state, the soul says, with conviction, "I am the form of peace, love, power and bliss."

When this experience begins to pervade your image of yourself, you will never again find yourself saying things like,

"I am upset, I am angry, I am unhappy."

Why not?

Because this word "I" changes completely.

II   Who Am I?

Whenever I use this word "I," I know exactly who I am talking about.

I, the soul, am a very wonderful, sweet point of pure light.

You can have this same experience.

There is such a difference between this soul conscious experience of yourself, and the other worldly one based on body consciousness.

The World

Meditation

I, the eternal soul, a beautiful point of sparkling light, am. As the soul again becomes aware of "who I am," something else changes, and that is the awareness of "what is mine." There are three aspects to this.

III What Is Mine

The first is that from the point of view of eternity (which is the perspective of the soul), nothing can really be "mine." People who I think belong to me, in fact, do not. They cannot.

They are also souls, in bodies, playing out their parts, like actors on a stage. They will all ultimately leave those bodies and move on to play different parts.

The second aspect is about possessions. From the eternal point of view, all material possessions are perishable. Therefore, any material attainments are illusory; that is, temporary—at best.

The third aspect is more subtle, and it concerns your body. The body, because it is made of matter, can also be considered a material possession . . .

Although it is true that, because it is matter, it will never be a permanent possession; nevertheless, it is worth thinking of the body in the same way that you look at other so-called possessions.

It is worth thinking of the body as "my body" . . . as in, "This is my body"? Why?

Because it reinforces the truth.

The truth is not, "I am a body and I have a soul," but rather, "I am a soul and here is my body. The body is *mine*."

It is something I own—or at least am using in trust . . .

The point is, the body is a possession; it is not me.

IV The Third Eye

Understanding and experiencing this true "I" and "mine" is the basis of spirituality. It is also known as using the third eye.

Through this eye/I, you can see your true, original Self. Through the two physical eyes, you will never be able to see this Self. Through the physical eyes, you can see the bodies of others, the world, the sky, the earth . . . all those things.

However, you, the eternal soul—that you will only be able to see by knowing your Self.

So the third eye is all about the awareness of "who I am" and "what is mine."

Back in the early days, we used to say our school was an Eye Hospital and we invited people to come and have their eye/I checked.

So people would come and in one sitting their third eye would open!

In other words, they could understand and feel that original, pure state of the soul.

It takes a long time to do a physical eye operation, but spiritual eye operations are successful in almost no time at all.

The eye/I is opened and you can see! It feels so good! You're alive!

&

What is the basis of a good spiritual education?

First of all, you need to know who you are. You need to know that you are a spiritual being, distinct from the body; that when we say "soul," we are talking about something completely separate from the body.

I I Am a Soul

Knowing yourself as a soul gives you a spiritual identity.

This then needs to become the consciousness from which you operate in your everyday life.

It needs to be practiced, not just lodged somewhere in the brain as an intellectual concept! The benefits of this are many.

First of all, you will be able to start steadying the mind; that is, to keep it quiet. This in turn allows inner, spiritual power to develop.

The benefit in this is that not only will you start seeing your problems clearly, but you will have the strength to overcome them as well.

The awareness of your spiritual identity is developed by training the mind to remain in a state of inner attentiveness to God, at all times.

It is a state of inner silence, a state of great peace and nourishment to which the mind needs to return again and again, no matter what task it is involved in.

It is a matter of keeping the mind free from worry and being able to maintain that inner focus, no matter how much responsibility there may be.

II The One

The second thing you need to know is this: Who you belong to.

There is One who is Supreme; One who is God, Allah; One whom we all love.

There is One on whom our attention is always focused, in times of difficulty . . .

. . . One towards whom we all point our finger, in the same upward direction. There is One who is God. One who brings benefit to all, who uplifts all.

People of all religions belong to this same One, accept this same One.

And remembering this One not only liberates us from the wrongs of our past, but empowers us to do what is right, now.

III   The Law of Karma

The third aspect you need to understand is the deep philosophy of action; or, in other words, the law of cause and effect.

This is also known as the law of "karma."

The law of karma teaches us to perform only those actions which are elevated, so that our own conscience can agree that the only actions we are doing are those right ones taught by God.

What are those right actions?

Just as God is the One who removes everyone's sorrow and bestows happiness on all, so can we develop those same powers, so that we are able to do the same for others.

Nonviolence is the highest form of religion, and this awareness marks the beginning of an end to violence.

Let us reach for such heights that we become truly able to remove the sorrow and suffering of others and give them peace.

Let us finish any thoughts of violence, hatred, and even thoughts of dislike from within our heart.

Throughout my whole life, I can truly say that this is the instruction from God that I have always followed.

My experience is that if your feelings are of love, devotion and faith in God, then you can be assured that the rest is in God's hands.

What are the efforts I need to make on the spiritual path?

The first effort is to become true to yourself.

This is because, when there is spiritual honesty, it is easy to receive help from God. Taking God's help is the beautiful endeavor of these times.

However, only an experienced soul will know how to take real help from God.

I   Centered and Aligned

You have to know how to take His hand and place it on your heart and head.

This means paying complete attention to the quality of your thoughts and feelings, and grounding yourself in your identity as an eternal spiritual being.

This fills you with the qualities of your original divinity: peace, love, bliss and might.

Feeling God's hand on both your head and heart in this way allows you to stay completely centered and aligned with your highest self.

Even in the midst of total chaos—inner or outer— you are able to remain responsible for every thought, word and action.

The ability to act from such an elevated state of awareness, even in difficult situations, is proof that you are making the right efforts.

Blaming others and considering them the cause of your distress and unhappiness is carelessness. It leads only to feeling disheartened.

Keep the heart and mind clear, that is, honest.

Then your efforts will bring real success.

How can I assess my progress?

A good measure of your progress is the degree to which you have the power of concentration.

This means the ability to center yourself completely in your spiritual identity, to the exclusion of any other programming or conditioning.

The more deeply you understand the process of meditation and yourself as a spiritual being, to that extent you will be able to start looking at your own self.

You will also be able to break the habit of thinking unnecessarily about others.

This allows the power of concentration to increase.

Much is received through the power of concentration.

Because it cultivates the inner strength that real change requires, it is the real foundation of true transformation.

I Happy Relationships

To see how much you are really changing from within, check the caliber of your interactions with others.

To what extent are the vices of anger, greed and attachment decreasing? First they decrease, then they are actually eliminated completely.

The sign of this is that you start enjoying happy relationships instead of those that trap, limit or in any way bring you down.

Ultimately, you become free of all constraints.

Why do I often get headaches when meditating?

Many people get headaches when trying to meditate, even though meditation is a method to remove headaches once and for all!

If your method of meditation is to force your mind to keep quiet, when in fact all it wants to do is race around, then obviously there is going to be some tension in your head.

Headaches come because of trying to repress your mental activity. You need to know instead how to quiet your thoughts respectfully.

You need to know how to gently redirect your thoughts to that place of peace at the core of your innermost being. Then, there will be no more headaches.

There is no need to try to bring your mind under control through force. All you need do is start saying good things to your mind.

Talk to your mind.

Tell it the good, sweet, positive things of eternal truth.

This is the way to redirect your thoughts and give your mind strength.

It's not a question of controlling your mind or forcing it not to think.

It's not even a question of emptying your mind of thoughts.

Meditation is simply a way of teaching your mind to think the right things.

What is the role of the brain in meditation?

This is a subtle aspect, and so to understand the answer you have to make your brain subtle, too.

This isn't something to just listen to. You have to think about it, relate it to your own experience and verify it further in terms of the feelings you get about it.

I   The Divine Intellect

Think about a time when you were sitting in a very pure and powerful state of meditation.

If in that state, a pure and elevated thought arises—out of the blue, so to speak—what is actually happening?

Is it just the ordinary machinations of the brain continuing to function? No.

At that moment the brain, which simply operates according to your old personality traits, has been set aside.

And the divine intellect, given by God, has begun to function instead.

Cultivating this divine intellect, rather than the brain, is the task to undertake now.

Let the brain become still and quiet.

Even as you reflect on the answer to this question, do not use your brain.

Everybody is so clever in using the brain, but now teach the brain to be quiet.

This has been one of my efforts from the beginning. I have always made sure that I do not use my head, that is, my brain, too much.

A lot of energy is wasted by thinking too much.

I only allow my divine intellect to work, and even then, only for what is needed by God.

II Being "Touched" by God

Many situations come up that would normally require a lot of reflection.

However, I still won't spend a lot of time thinking about them.

Why not? Because God works by "touching" our intellects, and for this the mind can't be cluttered with a lot of thoughts.

When the mind is clean, that is when there are only the thoughts of goodwill toward all, the intellect can then catch God's "touchings."

Then whatever is needed will emerge at exactly the right moment.

What is needed is to just sit in silence and let the "touchings" filter through. It is not a question of battling over anything in your head, but of just letting it sit with you and feeling it.

This happens easily when the desire in the heart is to do only that which God wants you to do.

III   Spiritual Nourishment

Keep your attention on the divine intellect, not the brain. Mere thinking, especially the kind that just runs you into the ground, will not do the job.

Deep contemplation of eternal spiritual truths will.

This is what nourishes the intellect and, ultimately, makes it divine.

How can I increase my concentration in meditation?

It is true that many kinds of unnecessary and negative thoughts can arise while sitting in meditation.

It is also true that you need to become free from them all.

There is a connection between your general state of mind and the ability to concentrate in meditation. Being aware of this connection is the key.

I   The Connection

Distracting thoughts in meditation are often the result of a lack of attention on your thought patterns throughout the day.

If you are not in charge of your thoughts as you go about your daily life, this will be the situation when you sit down to meditate as well.

The first step in meditation is to feed your mind positive thoughts about your original, divine identity.

These are like tinder which, when accumulated, enable you to build a strong and steady internal flame.

If your thoughts throughout the day do not reflect a spiritual awareness, no stock of pure thoughts is being accumulated.

Sitting in meditation is then like trying to start a fire without the proper material.

It takes a lot of effort, without much reward.

II   Negative Thoughts

Negative thoughts are those which come from vices like ego, anger, jealousy, making excuses, blaming and so on. These are very forceful in breaking your ability to concentrate in meditation.

Negative thoughts are like quicksand. Once they begin, you just start sinking deeper and deeper.

It is very difficult to come out of this kind of bog. It is even difficult for others to pull you out.

But you must get out at all costs.

III   Saving Yourself

One method to save yourself is to think about any good meditation experiences you have had in the past.

Hold them in front of you like a rope for your mind to grab on to.

If that doesn't work—if you can't get that flame going—then seek the company of someone whose flame is bright.

Just spending time with someone who has that light will help you to come into it, too.

Do not be arrogant and think you do not need anyone's help.

Learn to recognize the danger of allowing negative thoughts to accumulate in your mind. When this is your mental state, understand that you are not in a position to look after your own self.

Whatever accurate, true, spiritual help is available, take it and come out of that state.

Otherwise, how will you ever be able to be of any help to others?

IV   The Root Cause

The root cause of negative thoughts is a lack of faith in yourself and in God.

The solution is to keep filling yourself with so much spiritual awareness that all distracting thoughts, and any upheavals in the mind that they cause, come to an end.

How many hours a day does one need to meditate?

People often ask me how many hours a day I meditate.

My response is that they would do better to ask me how many hours a day I don't meditate.

However, this does not mean that I am always sitting around in a meditative state, doing nothing.

It means that while interacting with others, and carrying out my duties and responsibilities, I remain involved in maintaining that link with God constantly . . .

No matter where I am, who I am with or what I am doing.

The basis of maintaining a constant link is to maintain your sense of objectivity in whatever you do.

This means to never allow yourself to get so engrossed or absorbed in something that you forget your principles and overall purpose.

Remembering these aspects allows you to maintain your link with God.

It allows you to keep God in whatever you do.

This link is absolutely necessary.

Just as the physical body is of no use if the spirit has left it, in the same way, of what use are my activities if I, the spirit, am not linked to God?

It is only when there is that link that you feel you are in God's company.

There is also the feeling that whatever you are doing is being inspired by God.

Actually, this is an easy formula for staying in the world and being responsible, yet remaining as carefree and joyous as a child.

5

THE ART OF LIVING

What is the value of honesty in today's world? How can I develop it?

First of all, let's understand what is meant by honesty.

To be honest means to be true. It also means being faithful and trustworthy.

The more you experience this quality the more your sense of its value will increase.

I Self Evaluation

Do you consider yourself to be honest?

One way of evaluating this is to see how much courage you have to talk to God.

If you are not true, not honest, whatever would you find to say?

So go ahead. Do it!

Right now, in one second . . . go and say something to God . . .

Did you do it? Did you say something? What did you say?

Did you ask Him for anything?

If your heart is honest and true, the need to ask God for anything is greatly reduced.

After all, is God not the One who knows us best? Would He not know what we need before we even ask for it?

An honest heart is so open and clean, it picks up from God whatever is needed before you have even asked.

II Developing Honesty

Honesty does not need to be developed as much as it needs to be identified within the self and activated.

You can start this process by checking what you go to God for.

God definitely asks, "Why did you come to Me? What do you want from Me?"

When God looks at me like that, I just smile and say, "Oh, my One, what do I need from You?

All I want is the honesty and truth that You have . . . that this should become a part of me, so that I can become truthful and honest, too . . ."

No matter what the experience of God, everyone would agree that God is Truth.

Therefore, at the very least, all should have the right to experience this Truth!

This, actually, is precisely the duty that God fulfills.

III God's Donation

God fills our hearts with the pure energy of true love, true peace and true happiness . . .

And the feeling on receiving it is, "Yes, this is what I was missing, this is what I was looking for."

And there is so much happiness— just as there always is on finding something you had lost long ago.

Finding something that you had been looking for over a long period of time always brings a lot of happiness.

IV Maintaining the Experience

So what exactly has been found? The virtues, qualities and principles we would like to live by.

These emerge as the natural expression of God's donation of Truth.

They emerge, we experience them and there is great happiness in knowing

That truth does exist, it is beautiful, and it is, thanks to the connection with the Source, once again being activated in me.

When there is this experience, there is only one thing left to do. And that is to maintain it in everyday life.

This means to work with the aim of bringing that level of energy into your every thought, word and action.

In other words, to remain very peaceful, pure and cool—an incarnation of patience and love.

V   Spiritual Study

This is what it means to take up a spiritual study.

It does not matter if you also have a job, other studies or other activities and responsibilities.

It's fine to continue these. Simply maintain these natural qualities at the same time.

Take up the challenge of being honest to your inner truth. It is not just in your own interest to do so. It serves the best interest of others, too.

Those around you need what you have.

It might take a little time for people to know you, to know the truth you are working from.

During this time, you may even feel that you are being taken advantage of. However, that's okay, too. Let it take time.

Consider it extra time for practicing your truth and developing your qualities to an even greater extent.

VI   Relationships

As your thoughts, words and actions begin to take on more of your inner truth, your conscience will start clearing up.

There will be fewer and fewer feelings of guilt.

It becomes easy to forgive and be forgiven. Relationships improve. So does communication.

When you are honest inside, you never have to worry about how to say whatever you want to say.

You don't need to think out your every move, working out whether others will accept you or not.

You simply say whatever is on your mind, and others understand you, easily.

You get along with everyone.

VII   Victory

With honesty, it is as if an inner mirror is cleaned up, reflecting back to you the perfect self within.

You see that you are nothing less than the perfect child of God. You understand who you are, who you belong to and what you should be doing now.

In the face of this, ego, anger and all other negative qualities accumulated in the soul are defeated.

This is not a small thing.

VIII   Happiness

Honesty produces nothing less than this level of success.

It creates a very special kind of happiness . . . an inner happiness which removes all your sorrows.

It enables you to remove the sorrow of others, too.

With the happiness of honesty, you will never again be touched by the negativity of others, even if they are purposely trying to bring you down.

The happiness of honesty creates very deep feelings of internal security. Nothing can influence you haphazardly any longer.

IX   A Place in God's Heart

When this has been your effort, and the negativity within you begins to lose its hold, God is also attracted.

The Lord is pleased with an honest heart.

Your efforts to make your heart honest, that is, to live according to your true qualities of love and peace, bring you close to God.

Those who become like God in this way are His true helpers.

In God's task of world renewal, only those with such an honest heart can be of help.

This is the way to win a place in the heart of God.

How can I bring real meaning and purpose to my life?

Many people in today's world have lost touch with the meaning of life. They have lost their way.

They do not even know that their life *has* meaning, or purpose.

Or, if they do know, they are not able to articulate exactly what that purpose is.

I Purpose

What is the purpose of life? What is the purpose of *my* life?

I started thinking about these questions at a very young age.

However, not many people take the time to sit and ask themselves such questions nowadays.

If they did, they would find answers . . . answers which would guide them to their highest potential.

They would find their purpose.

II Highest Destiny

Many people are content to just look around, watch the world and live out their lives.

Some parents even give birth to their children without being able to explain to them the purpose of their existence and why they are here.

Nowadays, even the education they give in school does not generally help children understand their purpose.

Purpose is a subject rarely discussed, even though the demands of today's world make it vital that we be guided by such clarity of intention.

All of the worry and fear on this planet is due to people not realizing their purpose.

If everyone were to address this their highest destiny, indeed the highest destiny of humankind, could be fulfilled.

III   In the Hands of Humanity

Once I was asked to speak on the subject of the future.

In my talk I explained that there are three kinds of people in this world.

The majority are those who worry about everything—the population explosion, the arms issue, crime, drugs and so on.

They are always worrying, and they don't stop talking about their worries either.

The second type never worry. They just sit back and enjoy life and that's it. They are not concerned about anything else.

The third type genuinely and honestly believe that they can give such direction to their life so as to actually have an impact on the direction of the whole world.

In other words, they are those who feel responsible for the future.

This is to honestly face the needs of our times.

It is God's task to transform the world, but how does He do this?

God gets His task of transformation done through the noble acts of humans.

So now is not the time for being careless with our life's aim. It is the time to take up our world responsibility, truthfully.

Now is the time to think of the world. We have to do something for the world.

For this, you need to start by seeing what it is *you* can do.

You should do it and then share your experiences with others. Share what it is that inspires you.

In this way, you make it easier for people to think about living out their lives according to their highest purpose, too.

How do I balance spiritual goals with worldly responsibilities?

It is important, even while on a spiritual path, to honor all the goals and commitments that exist in your life.

However, there is a secret to being able to cultivate your inner purpose and be responsible to the world at the same time.

I   The Inner Focus

The secret is to start with the inner focus, the very positive and pure state of mind that comes from self-fulfillment, or, you could say, self-realization.

The idea, then, is to use that kind of energy to fulfill all your other obligations.

It is a question of the caliber of energy that you bring to your aims.

Start with the understanding that your first purpose in this life is to realize and release the dignity of your divinity.

Then, let that experience be the driving force behind whatever else you do.

Here is an example. Peace is one of the main qualities of our divine truth.

For this reason, whatever time I have, even if it's just a few moments, I always try to reach for that truth and fill myself with that peace.

The feeling is that peace is being stored, or accumulated within. This is so empowering that, in fact, accumulating peace has become my favorite hobby!

This peace is then what I use to fulfill all my other obligations.

II   The Power of Truth

There is power in a quality of truth that is accumulated.

I have seen, for example, how the power of peace can resolve many kinds of difficult situations. It clears up conflicts.

I have also seen how this truth sharpens the ability to know right from wrong—for the self and for others.

My point is that, whatever we need to do in the world outside will actually be achieved much more successfully if it is fueled by the power of our inner truth.

So keep accumulating the power of truth within the self. This is actually a key to being able to accomplish much more in the world through much less effort.

∽

Is destiny preplanned, or is it in my hands to create?

It definitely is in your hands to create a good destiny for yourself.

The first step in this is to simply have the desire.

Then, by taking help from God, performing good actions and remaining honest and focused in your spiritual efforts, your destiny can become good.

However, the interesting thing about the concept of destiny is that, as well as being in your hands to create, it is also predetermined.

It is important to understand how these two concepts—usually thought to be contradictory—in fact work together for our exclusive benefit.

I   The Law of Karma

Adverse situations will come up in our lives.

Instead of being taken by surprise and despairing, we can remain steady and creative.

The understanding of predestination makes this possible.

To understand that a situation was predestined means to know that it had to happen.

Predestination also works hand in hand with the philosophy of karma, which reminds us that nothing happens by accident. ("As you sow, so shall you reap.")

It also tells us that whatever is happening is good.

You can believe this is true when you understand that there is a secret, tailor-made lesson for your own personal development in every instance of difficulty in your life.

When you understand that the various trials and tribulations of your life are predestined in order to guide you in your unique and individual change process, you pay more attention to what they are trying to teach you.

After all, for however much your day today is a result of seeds sown yesterday, your *tomorrow* will be the result of the seeds you sow today.

Understanding the concept of predestination and how it cooperates with the laws of karma will keep you in the driver's seat of your life.

II   Free Will

Whenever something difficult comes up for me, I have just two things to say.

Firstly, "Okay, this had to happen, it was predestined, it had to come"; and secondly, "Now let me rise above it and keep moving forward."

The first thought is the result of understanding predestination. The second thought comes from understanding free will.

Free will is a component of the philosophy of karma.

Both predestination and free will work together. If there isn't a proper understanding of both these concepts and how they work together, difficult situations will slow you down or even stop you.

You will get caught up in them, forgetting that every thought, word and action of yours, at every moment, is not only your choice, but it is also a seed *determining your tomorrow.*

When you forget this, then truly it is as if your destiny is no longer in your hands.

You forget that whatever is happening had to happen, and that your task is to move beyond it.

Your task is to continue to create your future.

III Keep Going!

I have a lot of faith in God, and also a lot of courage to do what I want to do, but from time to time my body falls sick.

I used to wonder how I could create my future with a body that didn't function properly.

However, since then I have understood that you don't even have to think about such matters.

The important thing is to just keep going! Carry on!

No matter what comes your way, keep planting good, right seeds for your "tomorrows." I simply say to my body, "Okay. You do what you have to do, and I'm going to do what I have to do."

The same thing applies on even more subtle levels. The people you interact with daily will criticize, complain, compete and so on. But why be affected?

Let them say whatever they want. You just carry on with what you have to do.

Because God and time are on our side, we can create as high a destiny as we want.

Take help from God and use time properly. Then your destiny will definitely be in your hands.

6

ON DADI'S PERSONAL JOURNEY

What does God know about the heart of a woman?

There is a saying in one of the scriptures which states that only God knows the heart of a woman.

Although it is verse from an ancient text, I find that it is relevant to the times we live in today.

It is also relevant to the predisposition of women, in general, to matters of spirituality and God.

The first aspect to this is that, for a long time, some areas of society have based their understanding of women on the subtle feeling that women can't think—that a woman's intellect is not very good.

This is not true, of course, but the idea was reinforced through a misinterpretation of another problem entirely.

This other problem, which has not been understood at all, is that women do not have much self-respect.

Their self-respect has been lost.

Because of this, the opinions of society have been imposed on women, who in turn have come to believe these themselves.

In fact, due to the lack of this one essential quality, women are easily influenced by anyone's opinion much of the time.

I   Broken Faith

In many areas of society, a woman's views are not really heard. In fact, she is hardly even seen . . . no matter how much she tries to express herself.

The feeling this has created in a woman is that she has been deceived by everyone: husbands, children, politicians, doctors, lawyers, teachers, even religious leaders . . .

The result is that women have lost their trust . . .

Their faith in others has been broken.

II   Feelings in the Heart

This is one of the reasons why a woman is often receptive to the love of God.

The feeling is that God alone knows her as she really is, that He alone understands the feelings in her heart.

Also, God is known as the one who uplifts the downtrodden. Because she feels misunderstood and mistreated, a woman is predisposed to the love He offers. God's love not only uplifts, it also validates.

The Art of Living

On Dadi's Personal Journey

III A Woman's Greatness

God knows about a woman's greatness.

A woman's greatness—or, you could say, the greatness of the feminine principle—is Virtue, especially the qualities of mercy, love and truth . . .

God knows that for her these qualities are like possessions and, if she wishes to, she can use them not just for herself or her immediate family, but for the whole world.

He knows that, if she wishes, she can be more than just the mother of her one family.

She can be a mother of the whole world—the family of humanity.

These qualities make a woman like God, the Mother/Father. Through these virtuous qualities, she is made His own.

IV The Real Gurus

God knows that there is nothing as important as a mother.

The mother is the one who sustains the family. God knows that the mothers are the real teachers, the real gurus of the world.

After all, is it not the mother who educates her children through her own example?

V The Role of Women in Today's Society

In these times of darkness and sorrow, a woman's role is a very powerful one indeed.

If she stays in her own self-respect and takes power from the Almighty Authority, she can give the message of God to all.

Not only can she lead them out of this darkness, but she can lift them into the boat of Truth.

And show them how to go beyond . . .

What upholds the dignity of a woman?

There are three qualities that I believe come quite easily to a woman.

They are: tolerance, real mercy and the power of truth.

These qualities serve to produce a very big, open and generous heart: the heart of a world mother.

The image of the world mother is significant in today's world.

She is the one whose only desire is to help others move forward.

No matter what the challenges that surround her . . .

I The World Mother

The foundation of the world mother image is the feminine principle, which is all about virtue . . . virtues like mercy, love and patience.

Virtues like these are exactly what the world needs most nowadays.

Of course, both the feminine and masculine principles are to be found in each and every soul. But it is this one, the principle of virtue, which will do the most service in today's world.

Because I am a woman in this birth, my character has been predisposed to these qualities from the beginning.

I feel that this has been excellent preparation for the fulfillment of my responsibilities to my spiritual family—the whole world.

II Courage

I have never had the thought that this is "a man's world," and that we, as women, cannot succeed.

However, in today's world, true success will require constant courage and complete honesty on our part.

If you ever do feel afraid or discouraged, here is a secret I would like to share with you:

Take just one moment of silence, go within yourself *and evoke your courage.*

Have the faith that you do have a solution, you do have answers, you do know what must be done.

Never let yourself be influenced by what others might be thinking.

Just turn inwards, emerge the wisdom that is within, and then do something with it.

You only need to start with that one minute, saying to yourself, "Okay, let me see what can be done."

We are never without the solutions to our problems.

It's just that sometimes we may have to wait a little.

Learn how to remain peaceful, and patient.

The answers will definitely come and at just the right moment, too.

How do you express your unique sense of self?

One thought I have always had since childhood is that my life should serve as an example in front of the world.

I never had any intention of wasting my life on ordinary things.

I wanted a life filled with unique purpose and meaning . . . a celebration of the greatness of life, nothing less!

I was not interested in becoming a leader who leads through a lot of external show.

I wanted to be a true leader, leading through the power of truth, honesty and purity.

I   Becoming an Example

When I was in my late teens, I had a very powerful experience of God's love, of God as Truth. From that day on, my life has primarily been dedicated to two aims: keeping God in my heart in order to fly in the way only He can make me fly, and enabling everyone to come to know this Truth, too.

I used to think that for this I needed to teach others and go around giving many lectures.

Now I feel that my first and foremost task is to keep an eye on my own self . . . be my own teacher and pupil, and in this way, become an example.

In the early days we were encouraged to follow the example of the Founding Father of our institution in this.

He never gave anyone advice that he wasn't prepared to apply to his own self.

This became a working model for me.

If you yourself haven't experimented with and applied to your own life the advice that you give to others, then that advice will not prove to be very effective.

II A Global Vision

As a child growing up, whenever I thought of the world, I always had the image and feeling of holding a globe of pure light . . .

This was a vision of a world in which there was no separation between East and West. It was just the one world . . . and I was holding it in my hands.

This vision helped sustain me in my aims. First of all, it created a feeling of being separate from this world . . . in it, but also able to be outside it, and "hold" it, so to speak.

This proved to be helpful in developing my relationship with God.

It helped me understand the difference between a limited and an unlimited perspective, and how you can only be of real help to others when your own mind is not trapped in the limited.

Remaining in an unlimited experience of yourself allows you to stay above and beyond the effects of a problem.

This makes it easier to see where the solutions lie.

My experience is that efforts such as these are capable of making your life very different and unique, in a most wonderful way.

What is the source of your sense of purpose?

I have always felt that, because human life is so valuable, it is very important to live it out with purpose.

The purpose of life at this point in time, according to the needs of today's world, is to set an example for others; indeed, to make your very life that example.

I Purpose

Our world cannot afford any further insult to the spirit of our humanity.

We must take up the challenge of ceasing to do that which defames our world family and God.

This is the purpose that I have chosen. Not for my glorification, but for the glorification of us all.

This has always been my very strong purpose, one which I would be ready to die for.

Some people are ready to give up their aim in life, that is, their sense of purpose, as soon as even a little difficulty arises.

They say that they can't continue; it's just not possible . . .

It is true that a lot of inner strength is required to accomplish an elevated task.

Tests to our purpose come all the time; there's no fixed date or hour for tests.

And often, there is no one to help.

Not even God's help is always available in the usual way. For example, I have seen how, in times of difficulty, sometimes God is in front of me.

But at other times, He isn't.

So then I look behind me and see Him there, watching me to see how I will act . . . as if God wants to see if I have my own courage and faith,

or if I'm going to be like a little child who just gives up.

II   Moving Forward

I always make sure I remember that this is my Godly, student life. In other words, I feel that in this life, I must always be learning.

If you keep yourself in a learning mode, it is easy to move forward.

It's only when you think that you've learned everything that evil comes. If you let evil in, you will not be able to pass the tests to your purpose.

You will fail.

I always think that I've got to keep moving forward. I don't even allow myself to look from side to side. Forward only!

Those who have the habit of looking around instead of straight ahead always get stuck.

Now is not the time for going backward or being left behind!

I always keep my destination right in front of me. This is how I know I will make it.

Everyone should have this kind of firm faith in their elevated and true destination. Then it will be attained.

There are three strong voices that I am careful to listen to at all times: 1) my own inner voice; 2) the indications of time; and 3) the signals from God.

All three of these voices are helping us to continue moving forward.

Part C

Parting Vision

ANGELS

Part One

Angels are not like human beings.

Their form may be human and they can also be young or old.

However angels, no matter what their shape or age, are always very beautiful.

This is why angels are loved by everyone, no matter what a person's religion.

Even if people don't experience God in their life, but they do feel the presence of angels, they are happy with that.

People feel safe when they feel that angels are protecting them.

I   Original Creation of God

Angels are never shown to have a mother or father.

The parents of the different religious founders are very well known. However, in the case of the angels, thoughts of parentage don't even arise.

This is because angels are the original creation of God.

This is my experience: I have a physical form; I have this physical body.

However, inside, I am a spiritual being, a soul.

And in that consciousness, I am the child of God alone.

II   Becoming an Angel

Is it possible to become an angel? Actually, whatever it is you want to become, you can.

University students aim to make something of their life. They study hard and get their degrees, no matter how long it takes them. Ultimately, they become whatever they set out to be.

For the past sixty years, I, too, have been studying.

I have been studying to become an angel.

This doesn't mean that you will have to study for sixty years! It has taken me too long . . .

All you really need to do is know yourself as a spiritual being, whose original parent is God.

This ensures an inheritance.

Then it is only a matter of re-emerging that which is inherent.

All you need is to really have that desire, "I want to become an angel."

III   The Experience of Light

There is another experience I would like to share.

Ever since I was a little child, I was looking for God, longing to have an experience.

At the age of nineteen that desire was finally fulfilled.

It happened one day while I was out for a walk with my father.

As we were walking, I saw Brahma Baba, the founder of this spiritual institution.

As I watched him approach I had a "vision" . . . an experience of light.

This experience of light was a very special, beautiful moment; one which finally quenched my thirst of so long.

In that experience, I was filled with the feeling of being with God . . . of having found God . . .

I had known Brahma Baba before he founded the institution, so I did not imagine Brahma Baba to be God.

My "vision" was a result of Brahma Baba's own efforts.

He had learned to recognize and understand the Supreme. This is what enabled me to have the same experience.

In that instant, I had the feeling of being completely separate from my body.

And I knew that although my physical father was responsible for creating my physical body,

I really belonged to this Light . . . the Being of Light . . . who was God.

I felt so much joy and happiness.

In that moment, my heart was filled with one feeling, "You are my Father. I want to become like *You.*"

IV   Godly Qualities

God has so many qualities: peace, joy, love, purity, strength, truth . . .

I had always wanted to have such attributes in my life; however, despite my devotion to God all those years, these qualities were simply not present.

Instead there was a lot of fear, attachment and worry.

Yet, as soon as I had that moment of recognition, as soon as I said, "God, I belong to You," it was as if those Godly qualities started to emerge within me.

That which was latent, again began to emerge.

All my negative tendencies left me.

I simply no longer felt that they were mine.

V Recognizing Myself

When I talk about seeing the light of God, it does not mean seeing a flash of light.

When the third eye of wisdom opens, that is also called light.

Light is also the light of knowledge, the light of understanding.

That light allowed me to remember, that is, to recognize, my own true self.

It also allowed me to remember and recognize my own true Parent.

VI Becoming Light

Experiencing the light of God means there is a sense of recognition inside. Something inside you shifts.

Understanding from deep within begin to surface.

More than understanding, it is as if a memory is awakened and you are flooded with the recognition of who you really are and what God is.

At that moment of recognition, you are no longer bound to the (lower) consciousness of yourself as a body.

You are released from that and you, too, become light.

Part Two

Once I asked God, "Did you find me? Or was it that after all my searching, I finally found You?"

The reply that came was, "You weren't searching for me all that much.

It was I who was looking for someone like you . . ."

I God, My Support

God does look for those with honest hearts.

He looks for those who have such deep love they make of Him their only support.

Can you imagine someone like this?

Someone who, at every level, has made the basis of their well-being, God . . . ?

What would such a person be like? How much strength and virtue they would possess!

And yet they themselves would say, "Yes, I do possess a good character, but I know where it comes from . . ."

II Character from God

Nowadays, those who have good character often have the arrogance of that, too.

An angel, however, has qualities that come from God. This is why there is no ego in them.

You will never see an arrogant angel.

Angels know that according to today's world and the time, there is a need for beings of character.

And they know who has given them theirs . . .

Part Three

Another aspect of those who become angels is that they have no desires, as do ordinary human beings.

Because they have claimed their full inheritance from God, all their desires have been fulfilled.

They depend on no one and nothing for their sense of well-being.

This is why angels are always shown flying with arms outstretched, wide open.

They are freestanding entities, self-supporting sovereigns.

I Our Potential

Recently, I was alone on a small plane and was able to watch everything that was happening.

As it took off, the wheels of the plane were tucked up inside; when it was time to land, the wheels came rolling out again.

This even happened with the steps. When the plane took off, the steps were folded up inside. When it was time to land, the steps were unfolded out again.

No support of any kind was required.

These little planes are totally independent.

Seeing all this, my thought was how we too must do the same.

Like those planes, we are also free birds—self-reliant and totally independent.

This is the potential of our divinity.

We should use it to become so well-founded in truth, that our very presence serves as a source of inspiration to others.

We can become those who make of our lives such examples.

II　Our Birthright

All you need do in order to fly is submerge your physical senses and go inside yourself.

This means to remember yourself as light: a spiritual, divine being . . .

It means to understand yourself within the context of a different, more subtle reality—a reality filled with light,

With you, a being of light, taking all might from the Supreme . . .

As a birthright.

III   Maintaining the Vision

We become divine beings simply by understanding, believing and accepting that this is who we really are.

Then it is simply a matter of showing the proof through feelings of goodwill for all.

You need only to keep a check on yourself, making sure that your thoughts, words and deeds do not become ordinary.

The flight of an angel is not a question of physical flight. Physical arms and legs are not required.

The attitude and vibration of a pure heart and mind do all the work . . . through the eyes.

Let your heart be clean and your mind peaceful. Then you will be able to fly . . . with your mind.

This is the joy of becoming an angel!

ABOUT THE AUTHOR

Dadi Janki is a woman of wisdom. Her life's journey has been a fulfillment of her early childhood longing to know and come close to God.

Dadi was born in 1916 in India to a devout and philanthropic family. She had no formal education beyond the age of fourteen, her studies being mainly of the scriptures. At the age of twenty-one she joined the Brahma Kumaris World Spiritual University and dedicated her life to the spiritual service of others.

Dadi campaigns for truth and works tirelessly for world peace. She travels worldwide, teaching and sharing her wisdom and deep knowledge of spirituality. She is a soul who refuses to set limits and boundaries as to what is achievable and, in so doing, inspires others to believe that they, too, can make the impossible possible. Recognized worldwide for the depth and insight of her lectures and spiritual classes, her words of wisdom have given wings to countless souls.

Since first arriving in London in 1974, Dadi has overseen the expansion of the Brahma Kumaris' work into more than seventy countries and is now the university's additional administrative head. Dadi is one of the Wisdom Keepers, an eminent group of spiritual leaders convened at United Nations conferences. She is also founder and president of the Janki Foundation for Global Health Care and vice president of the World Congress of Faiths.

ABOUT THE
BRAHMA KUMARIS

The focus of the Brahma Kumaris World Spiritual University is to help people explore their inner resources as a basis for developing their highest level of personal integrity and the attributes of leadership. This unique method of education in human, moral and spiritual values was initiated in 1936, and is currently being offered in over 3,500 branches in 72 countries.

Affiliated to the United Nations as an NGO (Nongovernmental Organization), in general consultative status with the United Nations Economic and Social Council and in consultative status with UNICEF, the University has organized three major international projects in recent years. These include "The Million Minutes of Peace" (1986), "Global Cooperation for a Better World" (1988-1991) and "Sharing Our Values for a Better World" which was launched in 1995 in dedication to the fiftieth anniversary of the United Nations.

Each of the University's 3,500 branches worldwide offers courses in meditation and spiritual understanding, as well as lectures and seminars on positive thinking, self-management and stress management. Courses and activities also take place in different areas of the community, such as hospitals, schools, prisons, business and industry.

All courses are offered free of charge as a service to the community.

International Addresses
Brahma Kumaris World Spiritual University

World Headquarters

P.O. Box No. 2, Mount Abu, Rajasthan 307501, India
Tel: (+91) 2974 38261 68 Fax: (+91) 2974 38952
E-mail: *bkabu@vsnl.com*

International Coordinating Office & Regional Office for Europe and the Middle East

Global Co-operation House
65 Pound Lane, London, NW10 2HH, UK
Tel: (+44) 181 727 3300 Fax: (+44) 181 451 6480
E-mail: *London@bkwsu.com*

Regional Offices

Africa
Global Museum for a Better World
Maua Close, off Parklands Road, Westlands
P.O. Box 12349, Nairobi, Kenya
Tel: (+254) 2 743 572 Fax: (+254) 2 743 885
E-mail: *bkwsugm@holidaybazaar.com*

Australia and Southeast Asia
78 Alt Street, Ashfield, Sydney NSW 2131, Australia
Tel: (+61) 2 9716 7066 Fax: (+61) 2 9716 7795
E-mail: *indra@one.net.au*

India
Pandav Bhawan
25 New Rohtak Road, Karol Bagh, New Delhi 110005, India
Tel: (+91) 11 752 8516 Fax: (+91) 11 649 7824
E-mail: *bkdel.shanti@globalnet.ems.vsnl.net.in*

North and South America and the Caribbean
Global Harmony House, 46 S. Middle Neck Road
Great Neck, NY 11021 USA
Tel: (+1) 516 773 0971 Fax: (+1) 516 773 0976
E-mail: *newyork@bkwsu.com*

Russia and CIS
35, Prospect Andropova, Moscow 115487, Russia
Tel: (+7) 095 112 5128 Fax: (+7) 095 112 5126
E-mail: *bkpd@vsnl.com*

Web site: *http://www.bkwsu.com*

Main Centers
United Kingdom and Ireland

London
Global Co-operation House
65 Pound Lane, London NW10 2HH
Tel: 0181 459 1400

Nuneham Courtenay
Global Retreat Center, Nuneham Park
Nuneham Courtenay, Oxon OX44 9PG
Tel: 01865 343 551

Edinburgh
20 Polwarth Crescent
Edinburgh, EHI l IHW
Tel: 0131 229 7220

Cardiff
8 Haxby Court, Felbridge Close
Atlantic Wharfe, Cardiff, CFI 5BH
Tel: 01222 480 557

Dublin, Ireland
36 Lansdowne Road, Ballsbridge
Dublin 4, Ireland
Tel: (+353) 1 660 3967

North and South Americas

The United States:

1821 Beacon St., Brookline
Boston, MA 02146
Tel: 1-617-734-1464

3221 E. Manoa Rd.
Honolulu, HI 96822
Tel: 1-808-988-3141

908 S. Stanley Ave.
Los Angeles, CA 90036
Tel: 1-323-933-2808

306 Fifth Ave., 2nd Floor
New York, NY 10001
Tel: 1-212-564-9533

4160 S.W. 4th St.
Miami, FL 33134
Tel: 1-305-442-2252

710 Marquis
San Antonio, TX 78216
Tel: 1-210-344-8343

401 Baker St.
San Francisco, CA 94117
Tel: 1-415-563-4459

302 Sixteenth St.
Seal Beach, CA 90740
Tel: 1-562-430-4711

99-13 Georgia Ave.
Silver Spring, MD 20902
Tel: 1-301-593-4990

Mind's Eye Museum
2207 E. Busch Blvd.
Tampa, FL 33612
Tel: 1-813-935-0736

Canada:

897 College St.
Toronto, Ontario M6H 1A1
Tel: 1-416-537-3034

Trinidad:

55-57 Pointe-A-Pierre Rd.
San Fernando
Tel: 1-809-653-3766

Introductory courses in meditation are offered at each of our centers throughout the country, free of charge. For more information, and the address of a center near you, please contact one of the above centers.

Angels